The Money Journal

The Money Journal

FROM THE MONEY MUM OFFICIAL

Gemma Bird

broad book press

First published in Great Britain in 2023 by Hamlyn, an imprint of Octopus Publishing Group Ltd.

Carmelite House
50 Victoria Embankment
London EC4Y 0DZ
www.octopusbooks.co.uk
An Hachette UK Company
www.hachette.co.uk

Text copyright © Gemma Bird 2023
Design and layout copyright © Octopus Publishing Group 2023

All rights reserved. No part of this work may be reproduced or utilized in any form or by any means, electronic or mechanical, including photocopying, recording or by any information storage and retrieval system, without the prior written permission of the publisher.

Gemma Bird has asserted her right under the Copyright, Designs and Patents Act 1988 to be identified as the author of this work.

Licensed and distributed in North America by Broad Book Press, an imprint of Broad Book Group, LLC.

ISBN 978-1737517863

A Library of Congress Control Number (LCCN) has been applied for and is on file with the Library of Congress.

10 9 8 7 6 5 4 3 2 1

The advice in this book is believed to be correct at the time of printing, but the authors and the publishers accept no liability for actions inspired by this book. The author is not affiliated to any financial institution. The contents of this book do not constitute any form of independent professional financial advice, recommendation, representation, endorsement or arrangement and are not intended to be relied upon by you in making (or not making) a specific investment, financial or any other decision.

Neither the author nor the Instagram handle, @moneymumofficial, are related to or associated with the charity, MoneyMum.

Contents

Introduction 6

Hiya! 8

How to Use This Journal 10

Gemma's Saving Quiz 11

Setting Savings Goals 15

Setting Happiness Goals 16

Your Budget: Working It
   Out and Why It Matters 19

Get Out of Debt Checklist 22

Gemma's Key Techniques 23

Month One 28

Month Two 40

Month Three 52

Month Four 64

Month Five 76

Month Six 88

Month Seven 100

Month Eight 112

Month Nine 124

Month Ten 136

Month Eleven 148

Month Twelve 160

What to Look Out for Through
   the Calendar Year 172

Acknowledgements
   & Resources 176

Introduction

Writing down your goals ensures focus and accountability.

Hiya!

Money Mum here! I'm so excited to welcome you to my official money-saving journal!

You all know how much I love saving money. My family is, hands down, the most precious thing to me in the whole world. But being in charge of my own financial destiny also gives me a priceless sense of security and strength, especially on those days when I'm feeling low. I've gained so much self-esteem and inner strength from taking charge of my money and really making it work for me.

Since I started my Money Mum journey in 2016, it feels like the world has turned upside down and back around. We've been through not only the Covid-19 pandemic, but a global economic crisis, with energy prices skyrocketing and the cost of living going through the roof. I'm not going to lie, I can't fix it! Times are hard, and sometimes really weird! The past few years have shown us that we just can't take stuff for granted and we don't know what's around the corner.

So, while I can't promise a magic money wand, with this journal I want to help you take control of your money, so that when hard times come knocking, you can feel confident about how you'll cope. I'm going to tell you everything I've learned, and walk with you through the next 12 months, to help you on your way to achieving your own financial strength and resilience. It doesn't matter what your goal is or how much money you've got or haven't got. Whether it's about paying for your dream wedding or just about making it to the end of the month in the black, this journal is packed full of amazing exercises, handy things to do, and old-fashioned good advice that will help you to get there.

Before we start, I want to give you a quick pep talk to really get you motivated. Ready? Here we go...

If you've read my other book, you'll know I always say that money isn't a secret recipe, it's a mindset. What I mean by that is that money and financial resilience isn't something you either have or don't have, it's an attitude. I'm not personally into manifesting; I know that in the face of tough times it's not going to cut the mustard as a financial strategy. But I do believe that taking control of your money, and feeling confident about how you will weather those inevitable storms, isn't about doing complicated math or getting that pay raise. It's about a vibe, about developing the attitude or mindset that helps you believe in your own abilities to do this. Because guess what, my friends? You totally can.

It's exciting, right? Yes, Gem! So go grab yourself a coffee, and your pen and paper, and let's get started.

How to Use This Journal

I want to give you a decent amount of time to map out your journey to financial joy, but saving money isn't only for January, so this is a journal that you can pick up at any time and make a big difference.

To start, I've written a quiz to help you work out what kind of saver you are and a budget planner to help you set up your own budget spreadsheet—vital if you are going to get serious about saving. Then I've outlined some key money-saving techniques.

In every month there's space to outline and review your monthly budget, and a Monthly Spend Tracker chart to track down every little spend—remember, it all adds up! In addition, there's a Monthly Savings Checklist with some fun tips that you can introduce into your savings routine at any time of the year. I've also included information about some of the issues that might be affecting you on your financial journey right now, from understanding investing to budgeting for a puppy or recycling your clothes.

Towards the end of each month, you'll find space to journal about how the past few weeks have gone. This could include anything that's been bothering you financially or mentally, anywhere you had trouble, anything you could do differently, and ideas about how you might want to make changes next month. You can also tally up how much you have saved at the very end of each month. Basically, every month is full of ideas, information, and support, to keep you on track with your savings, whatever the time of year.

We all have different lifestyles, and saving can be trickier at certain times of the year than others. So if you do want some seasonal guidance, I've also highlighted some of the things you can look out for as you go through the 12-month calendar. And if you ever get stuck you can always jump over to my Instagram and TikTok pages for more information, inspiration, and support!

Gemma's Saving Quiz

Are you really good at putting a few dollars away every month or do you struggle to get to the next pay check without going overdrawn? If you follow me on Instagram or you've read my book *Save Yourself Happy*, you'll know I'm all about ditching the payday loans and saving up for what you want in life. And I'm here to show you how! But whatever you're saving for, whether it's an amazing vacation, a new set of wheels, or a deposit on that first apartment, you're going to need to actually save for it! I can't do that bit for you. I know—annoying, right?

The good news is that like anything you want to achieve in life, identifying your strengths and weaknesses when it comes to saving can really help you out. There is no one-size-fits-all approach to saving, so you need to think about how you can get the best out of what you've got. Money is something we all talk about far too little—we just kind of go through life blindly earning and spending. When was the last time you really stopped and thought about the way your personality affects the way you spend and save, and considered how you might be able to change things?

To help you identify the kind of saver you are, and think about how you could boost your bank balance, I've put together a quiz over the following pages. It will only take a couple of minutes, it's a really interesting thing to do, and it will help you become more aware of what can help you in the savings game.

What type of saver are you?

1. **DO YOU HAVE SAVINGS GOALS?**

   A   Hell, yes! I am always tracking my savings online and setting new goals when I hit my targets.
   B   I put money in a rainy-day account every month by direct debit.
   C   Sometimes I save for stuff, but not always.
   D   Hahaha—no.

2. **WHERE DO YOU SAVE YOUR MONEY?**

   A   It depends on the goal I'm trying to reach. For short-term stuff like Christmas and holidays, I use the savings accounts with the highest interest rates. For more long-term goals like a house deposit, I go for stocks and investment funds.
   B   I transfer money to my retirement or investment account.
   C   In my Prosecco Fund piggy bank in the kitchen.
   D   In my imagination.

3. **IF YOU GET A BONUS AT WORK OR A BIG CHECK FOR YOUR BIRTHDAY, WHAT DO YOU DO?**

   A   I'll review my savings portfolio and decide which goal to put the extra money towards.
   B   I'll probably put it all into my investment fund for now.
   C   I'll put half into my savings account and spend the rest at TJ Maxx.
   D   Vegas, baby!

4. **WOULD YOU SAY YOU KNOW ABOUT ALL THE DIFFERENT WAYS TO SAVE AND DO YOU MAKE IT YOUR BUSINESS TO KEEP UP WITH FINANCIAL NEWS AND CHANGES?**

A   I'm a total savings nerd and am constantly checking rates and switching accounts to get the best deals.
B   I looked into it all when I set up my savings account a few years ago but I haven't done anything about it since.
C   I think you can get help to save with some accounts these days?
D   All I know is that interest rates are terrible right now so it's pointless saving.

5. **WHEN YOU THINK ABOUT YOUR MONEY AND DOING THINGS LIKE REVIEWING YOUR ACCOUNTS, HOW DO YOU FEEL?**

A   This is my favorite thing to do! I love feeling organized and in control of money, and I am constantly tweaking my savings set-up.
B   I quite enjoy checking my balances and seeing how much is in there—it makes me feel good.
C   I'm too busy to think about it all too much, TBH.
D   Pass me a bucket, I feel sick.

Your answers and what they mean

Mostly As? You're a MOTIVATED SAVER. There's not much I can teach you about savings, my friend. You're in control and you know exactly how to maximize your money. Keep it up! Just remember to enjoy the spoils of your hard work from time to time!

Mostly Bs? You're an ACTIVE SAVER. You're on the right track! You are saving when you can and you know the value of having a bit of money put away. But you could probably get more out of your stash if you take the time to do some research and get into the habit of switching accounts when it matters. Automating your savings will help a lot as well, so you don't miss out on the slow build of compound interest and adding to your savings every month.

Mostly Cs? You're a DORMANT SAVER. You know it's a good idea to save but truthfully you find money all a bit boring and confusing and you'd rather just not think about it. Am I right? It's great you're not completely switched off to the idea of saving, but with just a few changes you could really see your money grow quite quickly. Stick with me, kid—I'm going to show you how.

Mostly Ds? You're a NON SAVER. Uh-oh! What is going on here, eh? You haven't got any savings and you probably get to the end of the month being overdrawn and/or maxed out on your credit cards. Sound familiar? You definitely need to get your savings shizzle together, otherwise how are you going to get anywhere? But don't worry—I've got you! Keep reading for all the advice and simple strategies you need to get yourself on the right path.

Setting Savings Goals

I love a goal! You have got to have an endgame, people. Something that you can work towards and realistically achieve is going to hit all the right buttons in your brain's reward center and have you feeling positive and motivated. And we all want a bit of that, right?

So, the first thing to do is to set yourself a saving goal or two. They don't have to be massive, and you can have more if you like, but too many might be a bit overwhelming, so start small. And they don't all need to be a year away—you could decide you want to have paid off a store card in six months' time, or have at least $3,000 in your investment account by the end of the 12 months. The important thing is to write your goal down and keep your eyes on the prize.

Goal-getter's guide to savings

- **Be clear about your goal and what it's for.** A 'rainy-day fund' is nice, but an 'all-expenses holiday to Mexico fund' is way more exciting! Choose a goal you can visualize.
- **Set a deadline.** All successful people understand the value of having a plan and a schedule. Knowing how far you've got to go helps you break your journey down and makes it feel achievable. If you want a new car, set yourself a realistic date to get it, and work out how much you need to save every week or month. Sounds obvious, but it's easy to forget and end up drifting.
- **Create savings pools for each goal.** A lot of app-based banking services now provide a 'pockets' or 'pots' function that lets you put money to one side within your current account. Or maybe have two separate accounts working towards different goals. The more you can see (and feel) your hard work paying off, the more motivated you'll feel about carrying on. Simple.

- **Break it down.** If you've set yourself a deadline and have a clear visual of how things are progressing, you will definitely start to feel the benefits of taking things in stages. But if breaking things down into months makes saving feel overwhelming, break it down into even smaller chunks. If you're trying to save $300 a month, maybe thinking about it as $10 a day will feel more achievable. Make a packed lunch, take your own coffee, walk partway to work and—boom—you've saved your Hamilton!
- **Make it automatic.** The type of saver you are will influence this, but making the savings process automatic can be a game-changer. Set up a standing order or use a savings app that automatically rounds up your daily spending and puts savings away for you. If you're earning cash it's harder to do this, but try to make putting a bit aside as automatic as paying your bills and you'll soon find that saving becomes part of your routine.

Setting Happiness Goals

When it comes to setting goals, don't forget to think about overall happiness, and set goals for that too. They can be as large or small as you like, but try to make them achievable and specific.

Think about the short term as well as the long term. Small tasks that you can tick off every month will help with the bigger picture and your overall satisfaction. Review your goals regularly and note down things you have been grateful for at the end of the month. All these little details somehow bring everything into focus more. It's important to remember that money and saving should ultimately be about making you and your family happy.

My short-term savings goals

☐ ....
☐ ....
☐ ....
☐ ....
☐ ....
☐ ....

My long-term savings goals

☐ ....
☐ ....
☐ ....
☐ ....
☐ ....
☐ ....

My short-term happiness goals

- [ ] ....
- [ ] ....
- [ ] ....
- [ ] ....
- [ ] ....
- [ ] ....

My long-term happiness goals

- [ ] ....
- [ ] ....
- [ ] ....
- [ ] ....
- [ ] ....
- [ ] ....

Your Budget: Working It Out and Why It Matters

So many people bury their heads in the sand about budgets, and I get it. They can reveal some harsh realities! But a budget can also be the lifeline you need, to get out of debt or to save that all-important pot of gold. Seeing it all in front of you gives you the clarity you need to make this saving thing actually work for you. So I say, even if this sounds like the worst thing in the world to have to do right now, grit your teeth, give yourself half an hour of uninterrupted time, and focus on your budget. I'm going to help you do it!

1. By all means use an app or online budget planner but a pen and paper are really all you need. This is not rocket science, people! Turn the page for my budget template, but this process is always as simple as two tables logging Money In and Money Out.
2. Start to fill out your columns. I've added some of the most common entries to get you started but left lots of space for you to complete sections according to your needs too. Be honest and leave nothing out, no matter how small.
3. Subtract your OUT total from your IN, and what you are left with is what you have available to spend—or save. What if the figure you get is a minus? Run through the outgoings again and be really strict about sticking to the absolute essentials. If it's still a minus, then see page 22 to seek professional advice.

TOP TIP: Use this exercise as an opportunity to cut out any unnecessary spending. That direct debit that keeps going out for the meditation app you subscribed to that you never use? Cut it out right now.

MONEY IN	TOTAL PER MONTH
Salary or wages	
Side hustle or freelancing	
Tax credits	
TOTAL MONTHLY INCOME =	

MONEY OUT	TOTAL PER MONTH
Mortgage or rent	
Childcare	
Taxes	
Electricity and Gas	
Water	
Broadband	
TV	
Mobile phone bill	
Credit card bill	
Home or renter's insurance	
Life insurance	
401k or investment	

MONEY OUT	MONTHLY COST
Car payment and insurance	
Car maintenance	
Gas	
Public transportation	
Groceries	
School expenses	
Pet food and vet bills	
Birthday presents	
Subscriptions	
Clothes	
Kids' clothes	
Toiletries	
Family days out	
Meals out and takeaways	
Holiday fund	
Hobbies	
Charity donations	
Fun money	
TOTAL MONTHLY SPENDING =	

MONEY IN − **MONEY OUT** = **MONEY TO SPEND OR SAVE**

YOUR BUDGET 21

Get Out of Debt Checklist

I've said this before and I'll say it again: there is basically no point in starting to save money if you still have debts to pay off. Debts tend to cost more (in interest) than any savings account ever gives you. So you are physically losing money if you are trying to save while you still owe. The only time it's OK to save while you've got debts is if your debt isn't costing you anything (like a 0% APR credit card)—and even then I'd always recommend getting your debts cleared first, just for the peace of mind. Debt keeps me awake at night.

Everyone's debts are different, but here are a few general pointers to help you on your way:

- **Pay off your most expensive debts first.** High-APR credit cards and store cards are usually the worst offenders.
- **Switch lenders.** You could save some serious cash on credit card debts simply by moving to a 0% APR account. But remember this kind of APR is designed to lure you in and you'll need to move again before the regular rate kicks in.
- **Ask for help!** There is *zero shame* in asking for help with this stuff.
- **Look after your mental health** Money worries can quickly spiral and become all-consuming, so try to recognize when your relationship with money is causing you anxiety or starting to damage your personal relationships. I've always been open about my mental health and many people have great sucess with medication or therapy. Make sure you talk to your GP urgently if you are worried about your mental state.

Gemma's Key Techniques
NO SPEND DAYS

I always say saving's not only about what's coming in, it's also about what's going out. Sometimes you just don't realize how much you are spending, all the time. One of my favorite things to do to help bring my spending into focus is my No Spend Day. This a day when you just don't spend anything! Not a penny. Sounds simple, doesn't it? But it can be surprisingly tricky to do. A bit like eating a doughnut and not licking your lips.

On a NSD you literally can't spend any money; direct debits, standing orders and any other important automated spends that it would cause problems to pause are OK obviously, but nothing else. Got no gas? You have to walk to work. Got nothing you fancy in the fridge? Make something up with what's in the pantry—or, better still, invite yourself for dinner at your mom's. Sale on at your favorite shop? Tough! Clear out your wardrobe instead and see what you can sell.

You'll be surprised by how often you have to stop yourself forking out in just one day. But you'll also be very pleased with yourself when you work out how much you have saved in a single day, too. Schedule in a NSD now and get ready to save!

TOP TIP: Throw yourself a bone and do it on a quiet day when you know it won't be so hard to resist temptation. Do it on a weekday when you're at work and you haven't got plans, and try to make it a regular thing so you get used to the idea. My favorite thing on a No Spend Day is to give myself a pamper night: run a bath, do a hair mask, paint my nails. It's such a luxury to spend time on myself and it doesn't cost a penny.

Gemma's Key Techniques
MAKE MONEY DAYS

Once you've got a few No Spend Days under your belt, you can start to add Make Money Days to your calendar as well. No prizes for guessing what happens on these days! That's right, you're going to make a concerted effort to raise a few dollars.

Now, obviously, if you have a job you are already making money, but this is about going the extra mile to make cash on top of your salary or wages. For most of us it's about having a proper clear-out and selling all those clothes we don't wear any more on eBay or other platforms like Poshmark. Or if you've got young kids, maybe it's time to get that travel cot out of the spare room and list it on your local Facebook Marketplace. I truly believe that *everyone* has something in their house they can sell for a few pounds.

Schedule in a Make Money Day now and see what you've got that you can unload!

Gemma's Key Techniques
WHAT IS YOUR HOURLY RATE?

If you get paid by the hour, this shouldn't be too hard for you to work out! But even if you don't—maybe you're self-employed or you have an annual salary—it's easy enough to work out your hourly rate: what you get paid for an hour of your time.

To do this, divide your annual earnings by 52 to get your weekly income. (Make sure it's your earnings after you've paid your taxes.) Now divide your weekly income by the number of hours you work. (If your hours are variable, use an average figure—the average national working week is roughly 40 hours.) That gives your hourly rate of pay. Here's a simple example:

Annual salary $20k divided by 52 = $385 a week

$385 divided by 35 = $11 an hour

This doesn't need to be precise or accurate, as it's only an estimate. The point is, you are trying to get a rough idea of how much money you earn every hour. Once you have that figure in your mind, you can begin to ask yourself not only if you can afford what you are about to buy or order, but if it is worth an hour of your life.

Gemma's Key Techniques

CARRY OVER THE LAST DIGIT

So much of saving success is about self-discipline. But life is hard; don't beat yourself up if your savings haven't quite got off the ground yet, no one teaches us how to do this stuff! However, if you feel like you'll never stick to your saving plans, I've got a little exercise that can help you get into the habit without it being a chore.

Take five minutes at the end of each day to check your balance and, whatever the last digit is, move that amount into your savings.

EXAMPLE

Monday	$265	save $5
Tuesday	$241	save $1
Wednesday	$197	save $7
Thursday	$233	save $3
Friday	$142	save $2
Saturday	$91	save $1
Sunday	$136	save $6

In one week you've saved $25! That's $100 a month and $1,200 a year—just from moving a dollar or two each day.

TOP TIP: There are a number of 'robo-investing' apps that do something similar by rounding up your spending and putting the round-ups into an investment or savings. Check out Moneybox and Plum to get started.

Gemma's Key Techniques
CREATE A MONTHLY SAVINGS LIST

At the start of each month, I find it's really helpful to sit down and think about how the month is going to play out, money-wise. Payday should not be about splashing all your cash at Target and going out and buying all the drinks! You've worked hard for that money, so look after it—and it will look after you.

For me, it's about taking a moment to plan and make sure you're covered for whatever's coming up in the next four weeks and, crucially, how you can save some of that precious hard-earned cash of yours.

To help you get into the habit, I've written a Monthly Savings Checklist—you'll see it at the start of every month in this book. This gives you a few key areas to really think about as you start the month, and identify the upcoming opportunities for saving a bit here and there.

Remember, self-employed people: you must set aside an amount to cover your annual self-employment tax bill!

TOP TIP: Follow my suggestions for your Monthly Savings Checklist while adding in some of your own savings ideas, that are specific to your lifestyle and hobbies.

Month One

Don't have too much month left at the end of your money.

Monthly Savings Checklist

☐ **Review your outgoings** Check over direct debits, standing orders, and subscriptions. What can you cut?

☐ **Schedule** Book in your No Spend Day and your Make Money Day for the month ahead.

☐ **Complete your budget** What can you put away towards your goal(s) this month?

☐ **What's coming up?** Check over what's happening this month and how you can save money on it. Get into this habit now and try to do it at the start of every month. (See my key dates planner on pages 172–3 for further help.)

☐ TRY THIS: SWITCH UP YOUR TIMING
There are so many savings to be had if you are prepared to do things outside of the most popular or normal times. For example, if you love playing golf but struggle to find the green fees, opting for a late 'twilight' round towards the end of the day will usually halve the cost for you. Similarly, if you buy your Christmas cards and gift wrap in January when they are reduced, you can save loads. Buy clothes and Christmas gifts in the end-of-season sales and put them away for next year. Head to the supermarket at the end of the day and you'll pick up all the discounted foods. And, of course, using public transportation during off-peak periods is cheaper than during the rush hour. Next time you spend something, ask yourself whether doing it at a different time could mean it costs less.

Monthly Budget Review

MONEY IN	TOTAL PER MONTH
....	....
....	....
....	....
TOTAL MONTHLY INCOME =	

MONEY OUT	TOTAL PER MONTH
....	....
....	....
....	....
....	....
....	....
....	....
....	....
....	....
....	....
....	....
....	....
TOTAL MONTHLY SPENDING =	

MONEY IN		MONEY OUT		MONEY TO SPEND OR SAVE
....	−	....	=	....

Monthly Spend Tracker

DATE	DESCRIPTION	CATEGORY	AMOUNT
......	....	....	....
......	....	....	....
......	....	....	....
......	....	....	....
......	....	....	....
......	....	....	....
......	....	....	....
......	....	....	....
......	....	....	....
......	....	....	....
......	....	....	....
......	....	....	....
......	....	....	....
......	....	....	....
......	....	....	....
......	....	....	....
......	....	....	....
......	....	....	....
......	....	....	....
......	....	....	....
......	....	....	....
......	....	....	....
......	....	....	....
......	....	....	....
......	....	....	....

DATE	DESCRIPTION	CATEGORY	AMOUNT
....	....	....	....
....	....	....	....
....	....	....	....
....	....	....	....
....	....	....	....
....	....	....	....
....	....	....	....
....	....	....	....
....	....	....	....
....	....	....	....
....	....	....	....
....	....	....	....
....	....	....	....
....	....	....	....
....	....	....	....
....	....	....	....
....	....	....	....
....	....	....	....
....	....	....	....
....	....	....	....
....	....	....	....
....	....	....	....
....	....	....	....
		TOTAL =	....

Practice Gratitude

When was the last time you practiced gratitude? I don't mean saying thank you for something in a restaurant or a shop—that's just good manners! I mean, when did you last really think about all the things in your life that you are grateful for? We spend so much time thinking about the things we haven't got, or we think we need, that we forget about all the things we already have.

Scientists reckon that people who regularly practice gratitude, taking notice of the things they're thankful for, are happier and more content in their lives. It totally makes sense—if you can't be pleased with what you've got right now, how are you ever going to be happy when you get new things? Without gratitude and being truly thankful for what you've already got, life just becomes one big series of disappointments as you try to get the next thing, and the next thing after that.

So it won't surprise you to hear that gratitude is pretty major when it comes to money! When it seems like you're getting nowhere with your saving, or you're feeling like you're not where you 'should' be in life right now, taking the time to reflect on what you've got is a brilliant motivator and all-round mood-booster. And the great thing about gratitude is that it doesn't only need to apply to the big stuff. Regular practice of gratitude can be applied to almost anything and to any amount of money. For example, you can be grateful for the roof over your head or the car that you drive, but you can also be grateful for your toothbrush because it keeps your teeth clean and gives you a nice smile, and smiling at people makes you feel good about yourself.

You could try keeping a gratitude jar, where you write down the things you are grateful for on a little piece of paper and put it in a jar. Then you can take a piece of paper out whenever you need a small reminder of something to feel grateful for. How you do it is up to you, and there are loads of online resources to help you with practicing gratitude. Try it from now on and see how good it makes you feel.

My Journal

Month Two

What if you just stopped caring what other people think of you?

Monthly Savings Checklist

☐ **Plan your weekly meals** Shop for specific meals and reduce your food waste.

☐ **Scan it** Use a hand-held barcode scanner when you go around the supermarket, to help stick to your budget.

☐ **Do meat-free Monday** Eating less meat is good for the planet and your pocket. Factor in just one or two meat-free days a week when you shop and you'll really notice the difference to your food bills.

☐ TRY THIS: DETOX YOUR INBOX

All those emails promising deals and tempting stuff to buy can leave you feeling really fed up and put you in a position where you want things that you can't afford.

I like to approach my inbox like a pantry or the fridge—it needs regular clearing and cleaning, otherwise it gets all blocked up. Take five minutes to go through all your emails and unsubscribe from any brand newsletters or other promotional emails you are receiving that you don't want or need (that will literally be all of them, then!). Each one of them is trying to poke a little hole in your financial armor—don't let them! Once you've got rid of them you'll feel lighter and freer, without all that junk sitting in your inbox.

Monthly Budget Review

MONEY IN	TOTAL PER MONTH
....	....
....	....
....	....
TOTAL MONTHLY INCOME =	

MONEY OUT	TOTAL PER MONTH
....	....
....	....
....	....
....	....
....	....
....	....
....	....
....	....
....	....
....	....
....	....
TOTAL MONTHLY SPENDING =	

MONEY IN		MONEY OUT		MONEY TO SPEND OR SAVE
....	−	....	=	....

Monthly Spend Tracker

DATE	DESCRIPTION	CATEGORY	AMOUNT

DATE	DESCRIPTION	CATEGORY	AMOUNT
....	....	....	....
....	....	....	....
....	....	....	....
....	....	....	....
....	....	....	....
....	....	....	....
....	....	....	....
....	....	....	....
....	....	....	....
....	....	....	....
....	....	....	....
....	....	....	....
....	....	....	....
....	....	....	....
....	....	....	....
....	....	....	....
....	....	....	....
....	....	....	....
....	....	....	....
....	....	....	....
....	....	....	....
....	....	....	....
....	....	....	....
....	....	....	....
		TOTAL =	....

Know Your IRAs

There are all kinds of ways to save for retirement, from company-held 401(k)s to employee stock ownership plans (ESOPs). But if you want to have additional savings buckets for retirement, an IRA is a great option. IRA stands for Individual Retirement Arrangement and having one (or more!) is a popular and reliable way to save your money. There are distinct types of IRAs out there nowadays tailored to suit your savings needs, so it's worth doing some research before you decide which one to open. Remember—you don't have to just go with the one your bank offers you as part of your current account! Here's an explainer of the most common options:

Traditional IRA

A traditional IRA is a tax-advantaged personal savings plan. You can contribute if you (or your spouse if filing jointly) have what is known as "taxable compensation." Contributions may be tax deductible if you meet certain qualifications, such as if you or your spouse are not covered by a retirement account at work. Speaking of taxes, any deductible contributions and earnings you withdraw or that are distributed from your traditional IRA are taxable. In other words, taxes are taken out when you make a withdrawal. Also, if you are under age 59½ you may have to pay an additional 10-percent tax for early withdrawals unless you qualify for an exception from the IRS.

Roth IRA

A slightly different flavor of savings plan, the Roth IRA is a tax-advantaged personal savings plan where contributions are not deductible but qualified distributions may be tax free. You can contribute at any age if you (or your spouse if filing jointly) have "taxable compensation" and your modified adjusted gross income is below certain amounts per IRS rules. Withdrawals are tax free if you make a qualified distribution per IRS rules. If you are under age 59½, you may also have to pay an additional tax for early withdrawals unless you qualify for an exception.

How Much Can I Contribute?

While you can hold as many IRAs as you like, there is a cap on how much you can put into them collectively. According to the IRS, as of 2023, the most you can contribute to all your traditional and Roth IRAs is the smaller of $6,500, or $7,500 if you're age 50 or older by the end of the year; or your taxable compensation for the year. Check www.irs.gov for the latest contribution limits.

My Journal

Month Three

Those that say they can, and those that say they cannot, are usually both right.

Monthly Savings Checklist

☐ **Affirmations** Start sending positive messages to yourself to keep you on track. Try once a week at first, and work up to once a day. You can write these on Post-It® notes, repeat to yourself in the mirror or write down in your journal!

☐ **Create online money pots** Check in with your bank about what online budgeting tools they have. Some allow you to section money off into different areas.—e.g. bills or personal.

☐ **Try Haggling** Call your phone, TV, and broadband companies and see what offers they can do for you to reduce your fees.

☐ TRY THIS: SWITCH OFF YOUR VAMPIRE APPLIANCES
Yes—they're really called that! I'm talking about all those machines we leave on at night—everything from our TVs and printers to heaters and phone chargers. These devices suck power even when you're not using them, and can add dollars to your energy bills without you realizing. The main culprits are TVs and games consoles left on standby, and phone chargers, which pull power even if your phone isn't attached to them! It's bonkers how much we are all spending on precious energy when we aren't even using it. Make a habit of going around all of your plug sockets at night and switch everything off. You'll sleep better knowing you're saving the pennies!

Monthly Budget Review

MONEY IN	TOTAL PER MONTH
....	....
....	....
....	....
TOTAL MONTHLY INCOME =	

MONEY OUT	TOTAL PER MONTH
....	....
....	....
....	....
....	....
....	....
....	....
....	....
....	....
....	....
....	....
....	....
....	....
TOTAL MONTHLY SPENDING =	

MONEY IN		MONEY OUT		MONEY TO SPEND OR SAVE
....	−	....	=	....

Monthly Spend Tracker

DATE	DESCRIPTION	CATEGORY	AMOUNT
....	....	....	....
....	....	....	....
....	....	....	....
....	....	....	....
....	....	....	....
....	....	....	....
....	....	....	....
....	....	....	....
....	....	....	....
....	....	....	....
....	....	....	....
....	....	....	....
....	....	....	....
....	....	....	....
....	....	....	....
....	....	....	....
....	....	....	....
....	....	....	....
....	....	....	....
....	....	....	....
....	....	....	....
....	....	....	....
....	....	....	....
....	....	....	....
....	....	....	....

DATE	DESCRIPTION	CATEGORY	AMOUNT
....	....	....	....
....	....	....	....
....	....	....	....
....	....	....	....
....	....	....	....
....	....	....	....
....	....	....	....
....	....	....	....
....	....	....	....
....	....	....	....
....	....	....	....
....	....	....	....
....	....	....	....
....	....	....	....
....	....	....	....
....	....	....	....
....	....	....	....
....	....	....	....
....	....	....	....
....	....	....	....
....	....	....	....
....	....	....	....
....	....	....	....
....	....	....	....
		TOTAL =	....

Fine-tune Your Budget

Hopefully by now you've got yourself a basic budget spreadsheet going and you've started to look at all the money you are earning versus all the money you are spending. If you haven't done this yet, head back to page 20 for a refresh of what a budget template looks like and why it's *so* important that you do one.

Now, once it's up and running, you can start to really fine-tune your budget and to sand off a few of those sharp edges! What do I mean? Well, for example, you might have a column that says 'Food' and in it you've put all your supermarket spending and food deliveries. Nice work! But what about that chocolate bar you always buy from the sandwich guy at work? And, come to think of it, the sandwich as well. Have you remembered to include these in your Food column? And where does the pet food go? Or have you got a separate Pets column? If you have, say, a Personal Care column, you might have all your shampoo and your make-up in there, but are you doubling up some of the costs here, because they're included in your supermarket shopping receipts?

Fine-tuning your budget is about being brutally honest with yourself and noting everything down so you can get the clearest possible picture of your money. It's also about being kind to yourself and realistic about what you need to cut back on versus what is actually quite important to you. If a really nice body lotion or shaving cream is an important part of your self-care routine, I don't want you to immediately cut it out because it's not the cheapest you can buy. It is so important that we look after ourselves in all ways—not only financially. So use this opportunity to think about what you are getting out of certain regular expenses, whether it's body lotion or wine or a newspaper, and consider their overall value, not just their price. Do you definitely want to keep spending on them? If so, what else can be cut to make room for them in your budget? You might find you save a few dollars you weren't expecting to!

My Journal

MONTH THREE

Month Four

Frequently check in with your goals to ensure that you are on track.

Monthly Savings Checklist

☐ **Fine-tune** Now you're a few months in, it's time to fine-tune your budget. Are there places where you're consistently under- or over-spending?

☐ **Review your insurance policies** Most people just allow their home, car, or life insurance to automatically renew each year, but you could be missing out on top deals. Note when your policies run out and check on a price comparison website. Usually the cheapest time to buy a new policy is three weeks before your old one expires.

☐ **Reality check** By the end of the first three months you should be able to see how realistic your budget is. If you are consistently overspending on your budget, then you could be in a debt spiral. It may be time to make some tough decisions by questioning and cutting out items that aren't 100 percent essential. See page 22 for getting help. You're not alone!

☐ **TRY THIS: CHECK YOUR BENEFITS ENTITLEMENT**
Whatever the circumstances, there are a lot of people out there who are rightly entitled to benefits, even if it's just for a short while. If you are struggling and think you might be eligible for help, it is worth going online and checking the government's tax credits calculator and its benefits calculators.

www.irs.gov/individuals/tax-withholding-estimator

Monthly Budget Review

MONEY IN	TOTAL PER MONTH
....	....
....	....
....	....
TOTAL MONTHLY INCOME =	

MONEY OUT	TOTAL PER MONTH
....	....
....	....
....	....
....	....
....	....
....	....
....	....
....	....
....	....
....	....
....	....
....	....
TOTAL MONTHLY SPENDING =	

MONEY IN		MONEY OUT		MONEY TO SPEND OR SAVE
....	**−**	....	**=**	....

Monthly Spend Tracker

DATE	DESCRIPTION	CATEGORY	AMOUNT
....	....	....	....
....	....	....	....
....	....	....	....
....	....	....	....
....	....	....	....
....	....	....	....
....	....	....	....
....	....	....	....
....	....	....	....
....	....	....	....
....	....	....	....
....	....	....	....
....	....	....	....
....	....	....	....
....	....	....	....
....	....	....	....
....	....	....	....
....	....	....	....
....	....	....	....
....	....	....	....
....	....	....	....
....	....	....	....
....	....	....	....
....	....	....	....
....	....	....	....

DATE	DESCRIPTION	CATEGORY	AMOUNT
....	....	....	....
....	....	....	....
....	....	....	....
....	....	....	....
....	....	....	....
....	....	....	....
....	....	....	....
....	....	....	....
....	....	....	....
....	....	....	....
....	....	....	....
....	....	....	....
....	....	....	....
....	....	....	....
....	....	....	....
....	....	....	....
....	....	....	....
....	....	....	....
....	....	....	....
....	....	....	....
....	....	....	....
....	....	....	....
....	....	....	....
....	....	....	....
		TOTAL =	....

Storm-proof Your Energy Costs

The early 2020s have been a bumpy ride for all of us. So many tragic events—it just goes to show that there's always going to be something around the corner that you can't predict in life. That's why I always say it's so important to have a decent amount in your emergency fund, so that you know you can manage when the unexpected happens. The energy crisis has been crippling for so many people, like families who have to choose between keeping the house warm and buying food. That's not right, is it? The costs of electric and gas went up significantly overnight, leaving all of us facing even higher household bills.

So, while I can't do anything about the causes of the crisis, I can help you to be prepared for, and to reduce the impact of, any future energy crisis. Not being a financial advisor, I'm not going to tell you whether to fix your tax withholdings or anything like that. But there is lots of great advice out there on this subject, and you should definitely look into it, as energy costs are variable based on your location and things change so much. Yet there's loads you can do to reduce your energy bills at home as much as possible and hopefully offset some of the rise in prices. This may sound obvious, but double-check that you are actually doing what you know already. We're all so busy it's easy to forget—here are a few tips to help you keep your bills down:

- Boil your tea kettle or make coffee once in the morning, then transfer the hot beverage to a Thermos®—you'll have hot drinks all day and save on your electric.
- Think about heating in terms of specific rooms, not the whole house. Adjust your radiators in rooms you don't use much, and use those old-fashioned draft excluders to keep warm air in. Keep yourself warm, too—get your thermal underwear and woolly sweaters on, and keep moving around to stay toasty.
- Switch off lights and close doors as you leave every room.
- Don't draw curtains over radiators—this just keeps the heat out of the room! Put a blind up for privacy and leave your curtains open so the heat can get into the room.
- Keep your eye on different providers and new deals via online comparison sites and switch as much as you can. Switching is easy these days and can sometimes save you hundreds of dollars, so it's always worth doing.
- Load your dishwasher to the max and keep it locked on eco mode.

My Journal

Month Five

Behavior is the hardest thing to change. It's a marathon, not a sprint.

Monthly Savings Checklist

☐ **Switch up your free exercise** Park runs, outdoor gyms, online workouts and dancing are all great options.

☐ **Take all your meter readings** Let your suppliers know exactly where you stand by logging online or phoning in. This is especially important when changing providers.

☐ **Out with the old** Schedule in a garage sale or a clothes swap night with friends. It's a great, free way to enjoy things that are new to you, and get rid of some old clutter.

☐ **TRY THIS: USE YOUR CREDIT CARD THE RIGHT WAY**
So by now you should know that I have a total phobia about debt and I never, ever encourage anyone to take out loans or credit cards when they are in debt. But if you are clear of debts and feel you have the right mindset to manage credit appropriately, a credit card can be a great way to earn freebies and sometimes even free cash. The key to getting the most out of a credit card is to use it in the right way. Pay your balance off every month and don't let what you owe build up—that's how you get the free benefits. I always pay my tax bill in one go with a credit card and get air miles for it. Just be sure you are in a position, mentally and financially, to pay your balance off every month. I'm not a financial advisor, so, as always, do your research before you take out any credit card or loan.

Monthly Budget Review

MONEY IN	TOTAL PER MONTH
....	....
....	....
....	....
TOTAL MONTHLY INCOME =	

MONEY OUT	TOTAL PER MONTH
....	....
....	....
....	....
....	....
....	....
....	....
....	....
....	....
....	....
....	....
....	....
TOTAL MONTHLY SPENDING =	

MONEY IN		MONEY OUT		MONEY TO SPEND OR SAVE
....	−	....	=	....

MONTH FIVE

Monthly Spend Tracker

DATE	DESCRIPTION	CATEGORY	AMOUNT

DATE	DESCRIPTION	CATEGORY	AMOUNT
....	....	....	....
....	....	....	....
....	....	....	....
....	....	....	....
....	....	....	....
....	....	....	....
....	....	....	....
....	....	....	....
....	....	....	....
....	....	....	....
....	....	....	....
....	....	....	....
....	....	....	....
....	....	....	....
....	....	....	....
....	....	....	....
....	....	....	....
....	....	....	....
....	....	....	....
....	....	....	....
....	....	....	....
....	....	....	....
....	....	....	....
....	....	....	....
		TOTAL =	....

Negotiate a Better Salary

(aka Know Your Worth)

How many of us feel we work our socks off, only to be under-appreciated when it comes to our pay? If you go to work and feel you are regularly going above and beyond your role, then you can and should ask for a pay raise! Even if you do get regular salary increases without asking for them, it can sometimes be worth asking for that little bit extra, especially if you feel you have been putting in the hours. And especially if you are a woman—the gender pay gap is still there, and studies show that when people *do* ask for a pay raise, men tend to be more successful than women. So it's really important that we women keep pushing to close the gap! Remember: Employers want to keep good staff and, as far as I know, no one ever got fired for asking, so it's always worth giving it a try! It's never an easy conversation to have, but here are a few tips to help you approach it with confidence:

- Choose your moment. If you know the business is struggling right now, it might not be the best time. Wait until you are sure the company is in a good place, or if you work for a big organization, choose a time when things are going well for them. Even better, do it when you've just smashed a target or delivered a brilliant project and the sun is shining on you.
- Know your worth—literally. Research typical salaries for the job you are in and for the work you are doing. The more evidence you have that you deserve the extra money, the better.
- Ask for a meeting to discuss your salary. Be very clear about it and don't surprise your boss out of the blue. Some time to prepare will allow them to warm to the idea!
- Practice what you're going to say. Even write it down and say it in front of the mirror—the more familiar you are with what you're saying, the more confident you'll feel about saying it.
- Remind them of your successes, but also paint an exciting future—they're not only paying you for the work you've done, but investing in you and in the company's future.
- Feel proud of yourself for working hard and asking for the appropriate compensation. If it's a 'no' this time, don't be disheartened. You've shown your boss you're ambitious and you know your worth!

My Journal

Month Six

Be grateful for what you have. Not resentful for what you don't have.

Monthly Savings Checklist

- [ ] **Reward** Schedule in a halfway treat. See below.

- [ ] **Re-take** Have another go at Gemma's Saving Quiz on pages 11–14. Where are you now? What do you need to change?

- [ ] **Review** All your direct debits, standing orders, and subscriptions. What has crept up in the past six months?

- [ ] <u>TRY THIS: MAKE ROOM IN YOUR BUDGET FOR THINGS YOU LIKE</u>

  I know, I know, I'm always saying don't buy coffees and take your own sandwiches! But you know what? If there is something you love and get a lot of pleasure from—whether it's a caramel latte at Starbucks or a trip to the nail bar or the pub once in a while—then try to find the space and funds for it when you are looking at your budget. It's important to strike a balance between being sensible and avoiding being miserable!

Monthly Budget Review

MONEY IN	TOTAL PER MONTH
....	....
....	....
....	....
TOTAL MONTHLY INCOME =	

MONEY OUT	TOTAL PER MONTH
....	....
....	....
....	....
....	....
....	....
....	....
....	....
....	....
....	....
....	....
TOTAL MONTHLY SPENDING =	

MONEY IN		MONEY OUT		MONEY TO SPEND OR SAVE
....	−	....	=	....

Monthly Spend Tracker

DATE	DESCRIPTION	CATEGORY	AMOUNT
......	....	....	....
......	....	....	....
......	....	....	....
......	....	....	....
......	....	....	....
......	....	....	....
......	....	....	....
......	....	....	....
......	....	....	....
......	....	....	....
......	....	....	....
......	....	....	....
......	....	....	....
......	....	....	....
......	....	....	....
......	....	....	....
......	....	....	....
......	....	....	....
......	....	....	....
......	....	....	....
......	....	....	....
......	....	....	....
......	....	....	....
......	....	....	....
......	....	....	....

DATE	DESCRIPTION	CATEGORY	AMOUNT
		TOTAL =	

Getting the Kids Involved

My two favorite things are my family and saving money! So obviously, I'm all about getting the kids involved in saving money from early on. I buy loads of my kids' clothes second-hand and I never give them expensive toys under the tree at Christmas.

Being frugal with kids is one thing, but how do you actually get them to pay attention to money and start to think about saving? For me the answer will always be simple: plain old pocket money.

Pocket money dos and don'ts

- **Do** give children a set amount of money every week.
- **Don't** be inconsistent, forget, or give them IOUs. They will lose interest.
- **Do** use real coins. Especially while children are young, the weight and feel of coins in their hands is just as important as their value.
- **Don't** encourage them to spend it all.

- **Do** encourage them to save at least half. A piggy bank or a clear jar is perfect—I used an old coffee jar when I was a kid, because I could see the coins mounting up inside!
- **Don't** give them any more when they run out. The point with pocket money is they learn that money is a finite resource. Like wages.
- **Do** talk about their money with them and help them establish savings goals.
- **Do** use a pocket-money app as they get older and want more financial independence.
- **Do** incentivize them to earn more by doing jobs.
- **Don't** give them more than you can afford just to be the same as everyone else. If you are struggling with your own money, it's important to make sure all your bills are paid and there's food on the table first!

My Journal

Month Seven

We are the products of our daily habits.

Monthly Savings Checklist

☐ **Take up a new free hobby** There are online courses for just about everything these days. Learn a handy skill and you could even save on labor costs for home repairs and such.

☐ **Do-it-yourself** Obviously when it comes to the important stuff such as electrical and gas maintenance, you should always use a professional. But there are plenty of jobs you could try for yourself—they could save you hundreds of dollars, and give you that all-important dopamine hit that comes when you complete a task you are proud of. Paint tiles with tile paint for a new look at half the cost. Pick up paint for small jobs at your local recycling center. Plant hedges in your garden instead of fences—they cost less and are better for the environment.

☐ **Be loyal** Monitor the companies you use most and consider taking out a loyalty card. Check out my Instagram for some great, up-to-date deals.

☐ TRY THIS: JOIN (OR SET UP) A LOCAL LIBRARY OF THINGS
This is a brilliant way to share local resources while spending very little, or nothing. From borrowing garden furniture or swapping kids' toys, to even offering skills, such as giving music lessons or baking bread. The idea of a 'barter economy' has gained a lot of traction since the pandemic. What can you offer in return for something you want? Check out 'buy nothing' groups on Facebook, or your local Facebook neighborhood pages, to get started.

Monthly Budget Review

MONEY IN	TOTAL PER MONTH
....	....
....	....
....	....
TOTAL MONTHLY INCOME =	

MONEY OUT	TOTAL PER MONTH
....	....
....	....
....	....
....	....
....	....
....	....
....	....
....	....
....	....
....	....
....	....
TOTAL MONTHLY SPENDING =	

MONEY IN		MONEY OUT		MONEY TO SPEND OR SAVE
....	−	....	=	....

Monthly Spend Tracker

DATE	DESCRIPTION	CATEGORY	AMOUNT

DATE	DESCRIPTION	CATEGORY	AMOUNT
....	....	....	....
....	....	....	....
....	....	....	....
....	....	....	....
....	....	....	....
....	....	....	....
....	....	....	....
....	....	....	....
....	....	....	....
....	....	....	....
....	....	....	....
....	....	....	....
....	....	....	....
....	....	....	....
....	....	....	....
....	....	....	....
....	....	....	....
....	....	....	....
....	....	....	....
....	....	....	....
....	....	....	....
....	....	....	....
....	....	....	....
		TOTAL =	....

Lifestyle Creep

What It Is and How to Avoid It

I'd never heard of lifestyle creep until a while ago, but as soon as someone explained it to me, I realized: Oh yes, that is me! Lifestyle creep is basically what happens when you start to earn a bit more money as you get older, but, instead of feeling wealthier, you end up with less spare cash in your account at the end of the month. Why? Because your brain is telling you that you've got more money to play with and you are making spending decisions accordingly. You get a pay raise, but because you think you're loaded all of a sudden, you might start buying the bougie shampoo or eating out at more chi-chi restaurants. Or you might book longer-haul vacations and buy those expensive shoes you like. It's all very nice until you realize you haven't got any more money in your pocket than you used to! So, how do you combat lifestyle creep? For me it's about going back to the good old basics of saving. That means going over your budget again and seeing what new spending habits are popping up on your spreadsheet. And it means putting money away into a savings account on the day you get paid, so that you don't even notice it's there. And it means revisiting your savings goals—maybe you can bring a deadline forward or increase your target, now that you've got the extra coming in.

My Journal

Month Eight

Hard choices pay off in the long run, whereas easy ones pay off in the short run.

Monthly Savings Checklist

☐ **Don't forget Christmas** Check in on your monthly Christmas saving (see pages 34, 94 and 175).

☐ **Break up with a brand** Try switching down to the supermarket's own brand or a cheaper fashion or grooming brand and see if you can really justify spending on the branded product. You can always go back to the one you love if you're not happy in the new relationship!

☐ **Start a 'one in; one out' policy** Only buy or bring something into your home if you are remodelling, recycling, or throwing away something else.

☐ TRY THIS: CREATE A SELF-CARE MENU
We've all got the memo about self-care these days, haven't we? It's important to look after ourselves so that we can look after everyone else without falling apart. But self-care doesn't have to mean expensive treats for yourself. Increasingly for me it's about making time for myself, whether that's heading out for a walk or taking a bath—doing something that makes me feel better but doesn't cost anything and doesn't come with a guilty price tag either. You can make it more fun by writing up a little menu of all the free things you can do when it's time for a little self-care, then choose the one you fancy. You could include painting your nails, bubble bath and audiobook with candles, taking the dog for a walk, going cycling, or cooking a favorite dinner.

Monthly Budget Review

MONEY IN	TOTAL PER MONTH
....	....
....	....
....	....
TOTAL MONTHLY INCOME =	

MONEY OUT	TOTAL PER MONTH
....	....
....	....
....	....
....	....
....	....
....	....
....	....
....	....
....	....
....	....
TOTAL MONTHLY SPENDING =	

MONEY IN	−	MONEY OUT	=	MONEY TO SPEND OR SAVE
....		....		....

Monthly Spend Tracker

DATE	DESCRIPTION	CATEGORY	AMOUNT
....	....	....	....
....	....	....	....
....	....	....	....
....	....	....	....
....	....	....	....
....	....	....	....
....	....	....	....
....	....	....	....
....	....	....	....
....	....	....	....
....	....	....	....
....	....	....	....
....	....	....	....
....	....	....	....
....	....	....	....
....	....	....	....
....	....	....	....
....	....	....	....
....	....	....	....
....	....	....	....
....	....	....	....
....	....	....	....
....	....	....	....
....	....	....	....
....	....	....	....
....	....	....	....

DATE	DESCRIPTION	CATEGORY	AMOUNT
.....	.....	.....	.....
.....	.....	.....	.....
.....	.....	.....	.....
.....	.....	.....	.....
.....	.....	.....	.....
.....	.....	.....	.....
.....	.....	.....	.....
.....	.....	.....	.....
.....	.....	.....	.....
.....	.....	.....	.....
.....	.....	.....	.....
.....	.....	.....	.....
.....	.....	.....	.....
.....	.....	.....	.....
.....	.....	.....	.....
.....	.....	.....	.....
.....	.....	.....	.....
.....	.....	.....	.....
.....	.....	.....	.....
.....	.....	.....	.....
.....	.....	.....	.....
.....	.....	.....	.....
		TOTAL =	.....

Establish a Passive Income

Have you heard of passive income, but you aren't sure how to get started? Passive income is where you are earning money without needing to do anything. Sounds like the financial holy grail, right? The most obvious type of passive income is owning something that you rent to other people—e.g. a vacation property or long-term rental. But you don't have to own a massive property portfolio to get started with passive income. You can use your existing skills and knowledge to leverage a new revenue stream! How exactly? One idea is to create an online course. Say you're brilliant at making clothes or putting on kids' birthday parties—those are skills that you can monetize by creating an online course and charging people for the information they need to learn your craft. You don't have to be a teacher or a professor to share your skills—it can be about anything! If someone wants to know about it, you can create a course.

Passive income doesn't happen by magic or overnight, so you need to lay foundations, do your research, and make sure it's something you can deliver on. And you should always see it as a side hustle rather than your main source of income—at least in the beginning! Go jump on Google and see what kind of passive income you can start to generate.

My Journal

MONTH EIGHT

Month Nine

You can't change others. You can only change your reaction to them.

Monthly Savings Checklist

☐ **Be mindful** Take five minutes every day to reflect on your money habits and where they come from. Learn to notice, and sit with, your feelings about money.

☐ **Give back** Try volunteering, or random acts of kindness when out and about, or even simply passing on a bit of love on social media—you never know what effect it will have on your saving habits. Good vibes are free and they never sell out.

☐ **Switch off** Try taking a month's break from social media.

☐ TRY THIS: TAKE A WORKATION
These are exactly what they sound like—a mix of work and vacation. Pack your laptop and head to your favorite city or coastal location (staying in roughly the same time zone as your colleagues is probably a good idea). Then plow through that to-do list with a view that isn't your own backyard. You get all the joy of being away, without losing any of the pay.

Monthly Budget Review

MONEY IN	TOTAL PER MONTH
....	....
....	....
....	....
TOTAL MONTHLY INCOME =	

MONEY OUT	TOTAL PER MONTH
....	....
....	....
....	....
....	....
....	....
....	....
....	....
....	....
....	....
....	....
....	....
TOTAL MONTHLY SPENDING =	

MONEY IN		MONEY OUT		MONEY TO SPEND OR SAVE
....	−	....	=	....

Monthly Spend Tracker

DATE	DESCRIPTION	CATEGORY	AMOUNT
…………	………………………………	………………………	………………………
…………	………………………………	………………………	………………………
…………	………………………………	………………………	………………………
…………	………………………………	………………………	………………………
…………	………………………………	………………………	………………………
…………	………………………………	………………………	………………………
…………	………………………………	………………………	………………………
…………	………………………………	………………………	………………………
…………	………………………………	………………………	………………………
…………	………………………………	………………………	………………………
…………	………………………………	………………………	………………………
…………	………………………………	………………………	………………………
…………	………………………………	………………………	………………………
…………	………………………………	………………………	………………………
…………	………………………………	………………………	………………………
…………	………………………………	………………………	………………………
…………	………………………………	………………………	………………………
…………	………………………………	………………………	………………………
…………	………………………………	………………………	………………………
…………	………………………………	………………………	………………………
…………	………………………………	………………………	………………………
…………	………………………………	………………………	………………………
…………	………………………………	………………………	………………………
…………	………………………………	………………………	………………………
…………	………………………………	………………………	………………………
…………	………………………………	………………………	………………………
…………	………………………………	………………………	………………………

DATE	DESCRIPTION	CATEGORY	AMOUNT
....	....	....	....
....	....	....	....
....	....	....	....
....	....	....	....
....	....	....	....
....	....	....	....
....	....	....	....
....	....	....	....
....	....	....	....
....	....	....	....
....	....	....	....
....	....	....	....
....	....	....	....
....	....	....	....
....	....	....	....
....	....	....	....
....	....	....	....
....	....	....	....
....	....	....	....
....	....	....	....
....	....	....	....
....	....	....	....
		TOTAL =	....

MONTH NINE

Pet Subjects

Budgeting for a Furry Friend

We are a nation of animal lovers. According to the ASPCA, over 23 million American households adopted a pet during the Covid-19 pandemic. Americans spent around $50 billion a year on non-medical pet goods. I love animals and I know so many people who get so much from their dogs—not only the love and companionship, but the exercise and the fun. But I am always amazed by how many people take on a dog without really thinking about the costs involved over their lifetime. Hundreds of thousands of puppies have been returned to rescue shelters after the lockdowns, as people have struggled to afford the costs of keeping an animal. So let's take a look at some of the things you need to consider before you bring that cute puppy home.

- **Breed**: Some breeds, such as French Bulldogs, are extremely fashionable and can cost thousands of dollars to buy. But because they're so popular, they can also become the victims of puppy farming and can end up with all sorts of health problems due to irresponsible breeding. Always go through a proper breeder or a rescue center, where you know everything is above board.

- **Food**: Pet food, whether it's for a Chihuahua or a Great Dane, is another substantial expense in your budget, so be sure you've got the money to spare before you sign up.
- **Vet bills**: This is major, guys. Puppies need vaccinations and annual boosters, plus regular flea and worming treatments. That's before anything goes wrong with them. Be sure you know how much all this costs, and get some pet insurance so you're covered if something bad happens.
- **Accessories**: I'm not even talking about diamanté collars and fleece hoodies, I mean just their harness, dog bed, crate, lead, toys, grooming fees if they have a lot of hair…If you are already struggling to find the funds for your own grooming, you need to ask yourself if you can genuinely justify taking on the extra expense.
- **Daycare, walkers and kennels**: If you plan to go away, someone will need to look after your dog while you are gone. This can add a sizeable chunk to the cost of your travels, so make sure you've got room in your budget!

TOP TIP: As a rule, small dogs cost less to buy and maintain than big ones, but small dogs tend to live longer, so consider this before you take one on.

My Journal

Month Ten

*Success is consistency.
Consistency is success.*

Monthly Savings Checklist

☐ **Call your insurance agent to find out ways to reduce your car insurance** Some insurers offer a discount for having multiple accounts with them or for clean driving records.

☐ **Walking is cheap!** Identify opportunities for more walking and less use of other transport this month.

☐ **Start using a parking app** The YourParkingSpace app and similar ones like JustPark find you the cheapest option wherever you are. So you can choose where and how much to spend.

☐ **Check your drag** Take roof racks off your car and clear out stuff from the trunk! And make sure the air in your tires is at the correct pressure. Your car will meet less resistance as it travels and use less fuel as a result.

☐ TRY THIS: ASK YOUR GRANDPARENTS AND PARENTS WHAT THEY DID TO SAVE MONEY
This is such an eye-opener! Older people are full of great ideas when it comes to saving money, so don't write them off as out of touch. I love hearing about the things my grandparents did: they'd put on a sweater instead of turning up the heat; use egg boxes to grow seeds in; only boil the amount of water needed in the kettle; freeze sliced bread and take just a slice at a time for toasting. All really simple and obvious ideas, but they make total sense and over time will make a big difference to your budget. Ask your parents or grandparents to share their money-saving memories with you—it will make their day as well!

Monthly Budget Review

MONEY IN	TOTAL PER MONTH
....	....
....	....
....	....
TOTAL MONTHLY INCOME =	

MONEY OUT	TOTAL PER MONTH
....	....
....	....
....	....
....	....
....	....
....	....
....	....
....	....
....	....
....	....
....	....
TOTAL MONTHLY SPENDING =	

MONEY IN		MONEY OUT		MONEY TO SPEND OR SAVE
....	−	....	=	....

Monthly Spend Tracker

DATE	DESCRIPTION	CATEGORY	AMOUNT
......	....	....	....
......	....	....	....
......	....	....	....
......	....	....	....
......	....	....	....
......	....	....	....
......	....	....	....
......	....	....	....
......	....	....	....
......	....	....	....
......	....	....	....
......	....	....	....
......	....	....	....
......	....	....	....
......	....	....	....
......	....	....	....
......	....	....	....
......	....	....	....
......	....	....	....
......	....	....	....
......	....	....	....
......	....	....	....
......	....	....	....
......	....	....	....

DATE	DESCRIPTION	CATEGORY	AMOUNT
....	....	....	....
....	....	....	....
....	....	....	....
....	....	....	....
....	....	....	....
....	....	....	....
....	....	....	....
....	....	....	....
....	....	....	....
....	....	....	....
....	....	....	....
....	....	....	....
....	....	....	....
....	....	....	....
....	....	....	....
....	....	....	....
....	....	....	....
....	....	....	....
....	....	....	....
....	....	....	....
....	....	....	....
....	....	....	....
....	....	....	....
....	....	....	....
		TOTAL =	....

Tipping and Splitting

The Modern Dos and Don'ts

Eating out and going to the barber or beauty salon can be a nightmare if you don't know what the deal is when it comes to tipping. Especially if you're part of a group and not sure what you owe, what the tip should be and all that—it's enough to make me want to stay at home, let me tell you. Everyone's got their take on this, but as a mum with her mind on the budget, here are my thoughts:

- Many restaurants now add a service charge (10–15 percent) to the bill. If your bill has a service charge, there is no need to add any more tip to your payment. If it doesn't include service and you feel your waiter did a good job, then feel free to tip, but *only* if you think they deserve it. Tipping extra is not obligatory.
- If you're in a group at a restaurant and don't want to get caught up in big, messy orders of wine and shared plates, just

take a mental note of what you ordered and ask to pay your own bill separately at the end. You can even go up to the staff and ask to do this before the final bill comes if you want to. It is not compulsory to share the costs of the bill if you haven't equally shared the orders.
- At the hairdresser, it's common to pay a tip these days, especially if you have had a color and a cut. If you have had a really lovely experience and want to tip extra, 20 percent is the usual amount and it's OK to split the tip between the two stylists if more than one person helped you. Ask the receptionist to make sure they each receive half of what you are tipping. Personally I always think it's nicest to tip the person who has washed your hair, as they are likely to be on a lower salary.
- At nail bars and beauty salons there is also an expectation to top, and 20 percent is perfectly acceptable.
- Try to carry some cash so that you can keep tips separate from card transactions and can be sure that the tip reaches the person you are giving it to.
- Never feel ashamed if you can only tip a small amount. You are paying the full price for the service you receive—and you can always come back again and tip next time.

My Journal

Month Eleven

Happiness comes from within, not from a designer handbag.

Monthly Savings Checklist

☐ **Patch things up** Put patches over holes or stains, darn the tears in your jeans (if you don't want the tears to show—personally I love a ripped jean). Try vintage patches over old logos. You could even start selling items online if you get good at customizing things like this.

☐ **Look after your clothes!** They're expensive, so make sure you hang stuff up, and use a clothes brush, lint roller, or steamer instead of automatically chucking them in the washing machine. And make like Stella McCartney and air your denim instead of washing jeans every time.

☐ **Eco wash** Work out the cheapest time to wash your clothes. It is generally less expensive to use appliances at night, but check with your energy provider. Always use the eco cycle and low temperature settings on your washing machine. Hang your laundry outside to dry whenever you can and try using white vinegar instead of fabric conditioner. Yes! It really works and is much cheaper and better for the environment.

☐ TRY THIS: RECYCLE CLOTHES FOR CASHBACK
Now this is a big one for me! I love clothes but I also know that fashion is one of the biggest polluters on the planet. Retailers like vintage stores and consignment shops give you cash for your clothes or a share of sales profits. They may even take all textiles and fabrics to be repurposed for things such as insulation, carpet underlay, and toys.

Monthly Budget Review

MONEY IN	TOTAL PER MONTH
....	....
....	....
....	....
TOTAL MONTHLY INCOME =	

MONEY OUT	TOTAL PER MONTH
....	....
....	....
....	....
....	....
....	....
....	....
....	....
....	....
....	....
....	....
....	....
TOTAL MONTHLY SPENDING =	

MONEY IN		MONEY OUT		MONEY TO SPEND OR SAVE
....	−	....	=	....

MONTH ELEVEN

Monthly Spend Tracker

DATE	DESCRIPTION	CATEGORY	AMOUNT

DATE	DESCRIPTION	CATEGORY	AMOUNT
....	....	....	....
....	....	....	....
....	....	....	....
....	....	....	....
....	....	....	....
....	....	....	....
....	....	....	....
....	....	....	....
....	....	....	....
....	....	....	....
....	....	....	....
....	....	....	....
....	....	....	....
....	....	....	....
....	....	....	....
....	....	....	....
....	....	....	....
....	....	....	....
....	....	....	....
....	....	....	....
....	....	....	....
....	....	....	....
....	....	....	....
....	....	....	....
		TOTAL =	....

The Art of Gifting

Whether it's a birthday present for a partner, a baby shower for a friend who's expecting, or a little something to take when you go to someone's house for dinner, gifts and giving them are significant parts of our lives. But that doesn't mean you need to spend lots of money! There is an art to giving a gift and it's very much not about how much you have spent. Here's my guide to giving the best presents without breaking the bank:

- **Show them you know them.** Give something relevant to the recipient that says you get them. Avoid bland, pre-packed gift selections and boxes.
- **Small is beautiful.** Little things, ideally something useful—a favorite nail polish or a piece of stationery, say—wrapped with care, will always beat grand gestures.
- **Handmade or fresh is always special.** Think flowers, a plant, homemade jam, or cupcakes. All these things are cheap and very cheerful.
- **Use your words.** A handwritten note will have more impact than any gift, so always take the time to write a little card to accompany your gift. Your recipient will love it and the best part is that words are free!

My Journal

Month Twelve

No one is good at everything, but making those small changes can help you move in the right direction.

Monthly Savings Checklist

☐ **Review** Read back through your journal so far—what has worked well and what hasn't?

☐ **Start a slush fund** If you are saving more than you thought, you might be in a position to start a slush fund: a back-up pot of money for unexpected expenses.

☐ **Think about your retirement** Now that you're settling into a routine, it's time to start thinking longer term and looking at your retirement plans. Are you on track to meet your lifestyle expectations when you reach retirement age? Think about how you can maximize your 401k's potential. Try an online calculator to see what happens to, e.g., $20 invested per month over 20 years with a modest 5% return per year compared to $20 invested per month over 10 years with a modest 5% return per year.

☐ TRY THIS: IF IN DOUBT, LEAVE IT OUT

Do you ever go out for dinner and find yourself secretly wondering why you bothered? Maybe the kids bickered all evening, or the food was mediocre. Or do you ever go shopping and come home with something that you're not totally sure about? I think I'm pretty good at self-control, but sometimes I do both of these things!

Sometimes it's just more rewarding to say no. If in doubt, leave it out—I love this phrase. Next time you're in two minds about something, walk away from the purchase, don't book the table, don't add to the shopping cart. You might find you feel better off for not bothering.

Monthly Budget Review

MONEY IN	TOTAL PER MONTH
....	....
....	....
....	....
TOTAL MONTHLY INCOME =	

MONEY OUT	TOTAL PER MONTH
....	....
....	....
....	....
....	....
....	....
....	....
....	....
....	....
....	....
....	....
....	....
TOTAL MONTHLY SPENDING =	

MONEY IN		MONEY OUT		MONEY TO SPEND OR SAVE
....	−	....	=	....

MONTH TWELVE

Monthly Spend Tracker

DATE	DESCRIPTION	CATEGORY	AMOUNT
......	....	....	....
......	....	....	....
......	....	....	....
......	....	....	....
......	....	....	....
......	....	....	....
......	....	....	....
......	....	....	....
......	....	....	....
......	....	....	....
......	....	....	....
......	....	....	....
......	....	....	....
......	....	....	....
......	....	....	....
......	....	....	....
......	....	....	....
......	....	....	....
......	....	....	....
......	....	....	....
......	....	....	....
......	....	....	....
......	....	....	....
......	....	....	....
......	....	....	....

DATE	DESCRIPTION	CATEGORY	AMOUNT
			TOTAL =	

Beginner's Guide to Investing

Heard of investing, but have no idea what it is or where to get started? Don't worry—it's not rocket science, OK? Investing is basically another way of making your money work harder. Some people buy property, others save, and some people invest. The big appeal of investing is that it's linked to the stock market, so you have the potential to earn far higher rates of return than the standard interest rates in traditional savings accounts. The downside is that it is a riskier strategy—you might lose money before you gain any, and it will probably take time to really see the benefits of your investments. The good news is that as long as you are invested for a decent amount of time (say around five years—this is not a quick-fix savings strategy) and you take a sensible approach (i.e. don't fling all your money into a high-risk investment at once), then you should be able to see your money grow and reap the rewards. Like all things money, there's a whole bunch of jargon that can bamboozle the novice. Here are my top tips to get you started:

- As always, make sure your debts are paid off first.
- Use a robot app such as Betterment to invest for you. Some only require a few dollars to start, while others, round up your spending and invest tiny amounts for you. This is a great way to dip your toe in investments without having to do too much thinking about it.
- Funds are like big cooperatives of fellow investors all investing in a range of stocks; these are safer as the risk is spread. Stocks are where you pick your own investments in individual companies—I suggest you leave stocks to the experts until you know what you are doing.

My Journal

What to Look Out for Through the Calendar Year

I've written this book so it's easy to pick up and start saving at any time of year. But we all know there are certain seasons that can be more financially challenging than others, especially if you've got children. Try to use this chart alongside your Monthly Savings Checklist, to see what's coming up on the calendar and to make the most of all your new savings skills.

JANUARY: **Traditionally the month of de-toxing and getting fit.**
- **Do** de-clutter and list unwanted items online. Exercise for free. Buy reduced Christmas cards and gift wrap for next year.
- **Don't** join the gym or sign up for any other financial commitments to do with wellness, such as expensive meal replacements or subscriptions.

FEBRUARY: **The month of love!**
- **Do** cook a brilliant meal, make a card, have a night in with your besties.
- **Don't** spend a fortune; something thoughtful is more romantic.

MARCH: **Spring is in the air, but not much else.**
- **Do** keep decluttering, refresh your home with simple DIY, plant bulbs.
- **Don't** buy a whole new spring/summer wardrobe.

APRIL: **It's Easter and that means...chocolate.**
- **Do** make your own egg hunt at home with 'treasure' like coins from the penny jar and clues and challenges to find along the way. One Easter egg from you is plenty. Make an Easter tree with a branch from the woods and decorate it with ribbons and handpainted eggs.
- **Don't** buy plastic eggs to hang on your tree, or a plastic tree. Pick flowers from the garden and make your own decorations.

MAY: **Bank holidays and the first few glimpses of sunshine!**
- **Do** get your summer clothes out and sell what you can. Save searches on eBay for your favorite brands in the right sizes. Give yourself a home pedicure with foot scrub and nail varnish.
- **Don't** buy out the Lowe's or Home Depot for your new decking project then leave all the boxes standing in the garden all summer.

JUNE: **Only a few weeks left until the school holidays start!**
- **Do** take your vacation now if you haven't got children—it's much cheaper. If you have kids, start to plan your summer trips and think about how much you can afford to spend for day trips. Save vouchers and promo codes for theme parks.
- **Don't** book a vacation you can't afford. Many operators offer free installments, but if you can't afford to pay for it in the first place, how are you going to enjoy it there? Holidays are about time with loved ones. Think about where and how you can achieve that without the massive bill. House swaps and workations (see page 120) are great options.

JULY: **It's about to get hot!**
- **Do** stock up on ice cream for the freezer and you can usually get out of buying one for $5 from the ice cream van. Apply your own fake tan.
- **Don't** spend a fortune at the garden center. Garage sales and flea markets are a great way to pick up plants and other garden stuff.

AUGUST: **Summer is in full swing and most of us are either off to sunny shores or stuck at work or at home with the kids.**
- **Do** take packed lunches and reusable water bottles everywhere. Keep a bag in the car with some snacks and empty water bottles so you can fill up wherever you are. Create an area in the garden or on a balcony

for an evening sunset with a table and a couple of nice chairs—even when there is chaos going on inside you can instantly transport yourself to Malibu with a cocktail and a pair of sunglasses!
- **Don't** go overboard with barbecues—meat and fish are expensive, so ask your guests to bring a dish or something for the grill. People never mind bringing stuff, and it makes it more fun and communal.

SEPTEMBER: **And just like that! It's back to school.**
- **Do** buy shirts and school uniforms second-hand, either direct from the school or from your local Facebook pages. Buy minimal school supplies as children never actually need four highlighters and special erasers—you can always add stuff to their pencil cases as and when they need it. Discuss school lunches with your children and get them involved with budgeting and buying what they need.
- **Don't** spend loads of money on expensive brands for your children to wear at school. Brand names aren't important to children—we inflict that on them! Simple, affordable shoes and clothes they can move and play in easily are the order of the day. And don't drive in every day if you don't have to; carpool with friends where possible.

OCTOBER: **It's Halloween!**
- **Do** enter into the spirit of this spooky festival season. Children love the entirely free thrill of monsters and witches and trick-or-treating at night time. Make your own fancy-dress costumes. Bake spooky treats and play games that are free and simple to make. Peel some grapes and put them in a bowl to pass around—they make great 'eyeballs' to squidge! Carve pumpkins and use the flesh for homemade soup or pie afterwards.

- **Don't** buy ready-made costumes from the store. They're expensive and made of unrecyclable plastics—yuck! Don't buy loads of candy for trick-or-treaters. One candy per trick or treater is fine.

NOVEMBER: **Thanksgiving and the build-up to Christmas begin now in earnest.**
- **Do** plan to buy Thanksgiving groceries in advance to save on the basics. Make it a potluck 'Friendsgiving' so you don't do all the cooking. Get clear about what you want to buy on Black Friday—the deals will be coming at you thick and fast, so you need to be prepared. Have clothes swaps with friends to get glammed-up for the party season.
- **Don't** spend fortunes on expensive electronics or clothing, or get seduced by Black Friday deals. Stick to your list and get in and out quickly!

DECEMBER: **It's coming! Christmas is here!**
- **Do** get out the wrapping paper and cards you bought in the sales. Think about handmade gifts and gestures—hand-crafted items and homemade jams are so lovely to receive, especially when in beautiful packaging. Consider digital cards to save on paper. If you're hosting, ask people to bring a dish. Read Christmas stories to children and watch old Christmas movies. Do Secret Santa to keep gift-buying minimal.
- **Don't** spend all your money on nonsense for children's stockings. Don't expect too much from other people—we are all dealing with our own struggles and demands. Remember my Hourly Rate principle (see page 25) and apply it to your Christmas budget. How many hours of your life are you prepared to 'spend' on Christmas?

Acknowledgements

I would like to state my sincere gratitude to my phenomenal agents that are Spotlight Management - Alan Samuel, Ange Walter and Heather Rose for all their continued, unwavering support. You truly are life-changing people!

To Sarah Thompson for being such an incredible voice and force in this journal's creation

To Lauren Gardner and all those at Octopus for their belief and continued commitment in myself and this book. Such an incredible team!

To my husband, Adam, and my wonderful children, Brody and Bronte. You are always there for me! I love you! Thank you!

Lastly, and so, so importantly, to my loyal followers. I truly hope that that this journal will help you change where you need to change, help you remain consistent and help you succeed in reaching your chosen goals.

Resources

If you are struggling to cope, then please know you are not in it alone. There are a number of organizations and services that may be able to offer you help either with further money advice or with support and guidance on your mental health. Try one of the following:

Foundation for Financial Planning: www.ffpprobono.org
Advisers Give Back: www.advisersgiveback.org
Consumer Financial Protection Bureau: www.consumerfinance.gov
National Mental Health Hotline: www.mentalhealthhotline.org